Ava Gardner

Ava Lavinia **Gardner**, born on December 24th, 1922, Grabtown, North Carolina, U.S., was an actress and singer. Ava was signed to a contract with Metro-Goldwyn-Mayer during 1941, having appeared mainly in small roles until she attracted attention with her performance in The Killers (1946), opposite Burt Lancaster. Gardner was nominated for the Academy Award for Best Actress for her performance in Mogambo (1953), having also received BAFTA Award and Golden Globe Award nominations for other roles.

Gardner appeared in several high-profile movies from the '40s - '70s, including The Hucksters (1947), Show Boat (1951), Pandora and the Flying Dutchman (1951), The Snows of Kilimanjaro (1952), The Barefoot Contessa (1954), Bhowani Junction (1956), On the Beach (1959), 55 Days at Peking (1963), Seven Days in May (1964), The Night of the Iguana (1964), The Bible: In the Beginning... (1966), The Life and Times of Judge Roy Bean (1972), Earthquake (1974), and The Cassandra Crossing (1976). Ava continued to act regularly until 1986, four years before her death in London during 1990, at the age of 67. She's listed 25th among the American Film Institute's 25 Greatest Female Stars of Classic Hollywood Cinema.

Gardner was born in a farmhouse, with no running water or electricity, near the farming community of Grabtown, southeast of Smithfield, Johnston County, North Carolina, the youngest of 7 children. She was named Ava, after an aunt, Lavinia, because it sounded pretty. She had two older brothers, Raymond and Melvin, and 4 older sisters, Beatrice, Elsie Mae, Inez, and Myra. Her parents, Mary Elizabeth "Molly" (née Baker) and Jonas Bailey Gardner, were poor sharecroppers, cotton and tobacco farmers. Her mother was of Scots descent, while her father was of Irish and Tuscarora Indian ancestry.

She was raised in the Baptist faith of her mother. While their children were still young, the Gardners lost their property, so Jonas got a job at a sawmill, while Molly began working as a cook and housekeeper at a dormitory for teachers, at the nearby Brogden School. When Ava was 7 years old, the family moved to Newport News, Virginia, where Molly found work managing a boarding house for the city's many shipworkers.

While in Newport News, Jonas became ill, having died from bronchitis during 1938, when Ava was 15 years old then the family moved to Rock Ridge near Wilson, North Carolina, where Molly ran another boarding house for teachers. Ava attended high school in Rock Ridge, graduating from there in 1939. She then attended secretarial classes at Atlantic Christian College in Wilson for about a year.

Gardner was visiting her sister Beatrice in New York during 1941, when Beatrice's husband Larry Tarr, a professional photographer, offered to take her portrait. He was so pleased with the results that he displayed the photo in the front window of his Tarr Photography Studio on Fifth Avenue, which was seen by Loews Theatres legal clerk, Barnard Duhan.

Duhan often posed as an MGM talent scout to meet girls, as MGM was a subsidiary of Loews, having entered Tarr's to attempt to get Ava's number, but was rebuffed by the receptionist. However, Barnard said, "Somebody should send her info to MGM", which the Tarrs then did. Shortly thereafter, Gardner, who was a student at Atlantic Christian College, traveled to New York to be interviewed at MGM's New York office by Al Altman, head of MGM's New York talent department.

With cameras rolling, Al directed the 18-year-old to walk towards the camera, turn then walk away, before rearranging some flowers in a vase. He didn't record Ava's voice, because her Southern accent made it difficult for him to understand her. However, Louis B. Mayer, head of the studio, sent a telegram to Altman: "She can't sing, she can't act, she can't talk, she's terrific!"

Gardner was offered a standard contract by MGM then left college for Hollywood in 1941, with her sister Beatrice accompanying her. The studio's first provided her with a speech coach, as her Carolina drawl was almost incomprehensible to them. Following 5 years of bit parts, mainly at MGM, many of them uncredited, Ava became famous in the Mark Hellinger-produced hit film noir The Killers (1946), playing the femme fatale Kitty Collins.

Gardner's other movies include The Hucksters (1947), Show Boat (1951), The Snows of Kilimanjaro (1952), Lone Star (1952), Mogambo (1953), The Barefoot Contessa (1954), Bhowani Junction (1956), The Sun Also Rises (1957), and On the Beach (1959). In The Barefoot Contessa, Ava played the role of doomed beauty Maria Vargas, a fiercely independent woman who went from Spanish dancer to international film star with the help of a Hollywood director played by Humphrey Bogart, with tragic consequences. Gardner starred as Guinevere in Knights of the Round Table (1953), opposite actor Robert Taylor as Sir Lancelot, having also portrayed a duchess, a baroness, and other royal ladies in her films of the '50s.

Ava could be witty and pithy off-camera, as in her assessment of director John Ford, who directed Mogambo, saying he was "The meanest man on earth. Thoroughly evil. Adored him!". She was cast with Charlton Heston and David Niven in 55 Days at Peking (1963), which was set in China during the Boxer Rebellion of 1900.

The following year, she played her last major leading role in a critically acclaimed movie, The Night of the Iguana (1964), based upon a Tennessee Williams play, starring Richard Burton as an atheist clergyman and Deborah Kerr as a gentle artist, traveling with her aged poet grandfather. John Huston directed the picture in Puerto Vallarta, Mexico, insisting on making the film in black and white – a decision he later regretted because of the vivid colours of the flora. Gardner was billed below Burton, but above Kerr, having been nominated for a BAFTA and a Golden Globe Award for her performance.

Ava next appeared with Burt Lancaster, Kirk Douglas and Fredric March, in Seven Days in May (1964), a thriller about an attempted military takeover of the US government. Gardner played a former love interest of Lancaster's who could've been instrumental in Douglas's prevention of a coup against the President of the United States.

John Huston chose Ava for the part of Sarah, the wife of Abraham, played by George C. Scott, in the Dino De Laurentiis production The Bible: In the Beginning..., which was released during 1966. Gardner explained why she accepted the role in 1964:

"He [Huston] had more faith in me than I did myself. Now I'm glad I listened, for it's a challenging role and a very demanding one. I start out as a young wife then age through various periods, forcing me to adjust psychologically to each age. It's a complete departure for me, and most intriguing. In this role, I must create a character, not just play one".

Ava briefly tried to get the role of Mrs. Robinson in Mike Nichols' The Graduate (1967), apparently having called Nichols during 1966 to say, "I want to see you! I want to talk about this Graduate thing!" However, Nichols never seriously considered her for the part, preferring to cast a younger woman, Anne Bancroft being 35, while Gardner was 44, but he did visit her hotel, where he later recalled, "she sat at a little French desk with a telephone, she went through every movie star cliché. She said, 'All right, let's talk about your movie. First of all, I strip for nobody!'"

Ava moved to London during 1968, undergoing an elective hysterectomy to allay her worries of contracting the uterine cancer that had claimed the life of her mother. That year, she appeared in Mayerling, in which she played the supporting role of Austrian Empress Elisabeth of Austria, opposite James Mason as Emperor Franz Joseph I.

Gardner appeared several disaster films during the '70s, notably Earthquake (1974) with Heston, The Cassandra Crossing (1976) with Lancaster, and the Canadian movie City on Fire (1979). She appeared briefly as Lillie Langtry at the end of The Life and Times of Judge Roy Bean (1972), and in The Blue Bird (1976). Ava's last movie was Regina Roma (1982), a direct-to-video release. In the '80s, she acted mainly on TV, including in the miniseries remake of The Long, Hot Summer and in a story arc on Knots Landing, both during 1985.

Soon after Gardner arrived in Los Angeles, she met fellow MGM contract player Mickey Rooney, whom she wed on January

10th, 1942, the ceremony being held in the remote town of Ballard, California, because MGM studio head Louis B. Mayer was concerned that fans would stay away from Rooney's Andy Hardy movie series if they knew that the star was married. Ava divorced Rooney in 1943 due serial adultery, but agreed not to reveal it to avoid damaging his career.

Gardner's 2nd marriage to jazz musician and bandleader Artie Shaw was also brief, lasting from 1945 to 1946, Shaw having previously been married to Lana Turner. Ava's third and final wedding was to singer and actor Frank Sinatra, from 1951 to 1957, whom she later said in her autobiography was the love of her life. Sinatra left his wife, Nancy, for Gardner, their marriage having made headlines.

Frank was castigated by gossip columnists Hedda Hopper and Louella Parsons, the Hollywood establishment, the Roman Catholic Church, and by his fans for leaving his wife for a femme fatale. Ava used her considerable influence, particularly with Harry Cohn, to help get Sinatra cast in his Oscar-winning role in From Here to Eternity (1953), the role and the award revitalizing both Frank's acting and singing careers.

The Gardner-Sinatra marriage was tumultuous, Ava having confided to Artie Shaw that, "With him it's impossible... It's like being with a woman. He's so gentle. It's as though he thinks I'll break, as though I'm a piece of Dresden china, and he's gonna hurt me." During their marriage, Gardner became pregnant twice, but aborted both pregnancies. "MGM had all sorts of penalty clauses about their stars having babies", she stated in her autobiography, which was published 8 months after her death. Ava remained good friends with Sinatra for the rest of her life.

Gardner became a friend of businessman and aviator Howard Hughes during the early to mid-40s, the relationship having lasted into the '50s. She stated in her autobiography, Ava: My Story, that she was never in love with Hughes, but he was in and out of her life for about 20 years. Howard's trust in Gardner was what kept their relationship alive. She described him as "painfully shy, completely enigmatic, and more eccentric ... than anyone I've ever met".

After Ava divorced Sinatra during 1957, she headed for Spain, where she began a friendship with writer Ernest Hemingway, having starred in an adaptation of his The Sun Also Rises that year, Hemingway having successfully urged producer Darryl F. Zanuck to cast Gardner in The Snows of Kilimanjaro 5 years earlier, a film which adapted several of his short stories.

While staying with Ernest at his villa in San Francisco de Paula in Havana, Cuba, Gardner once swam alone without a swimsuit in his pool. After watching her, Hemingway ordered his staff: "The water is not to be emptied!". Her friendship with Ernest led to her becoming a fan of bullfighting and bullfighters, including Luis Miguel Dominguín, who became her lover. "It was a sort of madness, honey", she later said of the time.

Ava was also had a relationship with her live-in boyfriend and companion, American actor Benjamin Tatar, who worked in Spain as a foreign-language dubbing director. Tatar later wrote an autobiography in which he discussed his relationship with Gardner, though the book was never published.

Although Ava was exposed to Christianity throughout her early years, she identified herself as an atheist later in life. Religion never played a positive role in her life, as she stated in her autobiography Ava: My Story. Her friend Zoe Sallis, who met her on the set of The Bible: In the Beginning... when Gardner was living with John Huston in Puerto Vallarta, said Ava always seemed unconcerned about religion.

When Sallis asked her about religion once, Gardner replied, "It doesn't exist." Another factor that contributed to this was the death of Ava's father when she was a child, stating, "Nobody wanted to know Daddy when he was dying. He was so alone. He was scared. I could see the fear in his eyes when he was smiling. I went to see the preacher, the guy who'd baptized me. I begged him to come and visit Daddy, just to talk to him, you know? Give him a blessing or something but he never did. He never came. God, I hated him. Cold-ass bastards like that ought to ... I don't know ... they should be in some other racket, I know that. I had no time for religion after that. I never prayed. I never said another prayer." Regarding politics, Gardner was a lifelong Democrat.

Ava suffered from emphysema and an unidentified autoimmune disorder following a lifetime of smoking, two strokes during 1986 having left her partially paralyzed and bedridden. Although Gardner could afford her medical expenses, Sinatra wanted to pay for her visit to a US specialist, so she allowed him to make the arrangements for a medically staffed private plane to the States.

Ava fell badly a week before she died, having lain on the floor, alone and unable to move, until her housekeeper returned, to whom her last words were "I'm so tired". She died of pneumonia at the age of 67, at her London home, 34 Ennismore

Gardens, where she'd lived since 1968. Gardner was buried in the Sunset Memorial Park, Smithfield, North Carolina, next to her siblings and their parents, Jonas (1878–1938) and Molly Gardner (1883–1943). The town of Smithfield has an Ava Gardner Museum.

During the last few years of her life, Ava asked Peter Evans to ghostwrite her autobiography, stating, "I either write the book or sell the jewels." Despite meeting with Evans frequently, and approving of most of his copy, Gardner eventually learned that Peter, along with the BBC, had once been sued by her ex-husband Frank Sinatra, so her friendship with Evans cooled, who left the project. Peter's notes and sections of his draft of Ava's autobiography, which he based on their taped conversations, were published in the book Ava Gardner: The Secret Conversations, following Evans's death during 2012.

Gardner was nominated for an Academy Award for Mogambo (1953), the award having been won by Audrey Hepburn for Roman Holiday. Her performance as Maxine Faulk in The Night of the Iguana (1964) was well reviewed, being nominated for a BAFTA Award and a Golden Globe, having also won the San Sebastián Prize in 1964 for best actress.

Ava has been portrayed by Marcia Gay Harden in the TV miniseries, Sinatra during 1992, Deborah Kara Unger in HBO's TV movie The Rat Pack in 1998, Kate Beckinsale in the Howard Hughes biopic The Aviator (2004), and Anna Drijver in the Italian TV film Walter Chiari – Fino all'ultima risata (2012). Surprisingly, for a Martin Scorsese movie, The Aviator had a chronological error, depicting Hughes meeting Gardner at the premiere of the movie The Women (1939)—an event that occurred two years before her arrival in Hollywood. The 2018 Spanish TV series, Arde Madrid, was a comedy-drama with thriller elements based on the events of Ava's life in Francoist Spain, in which she was portrayed by Debi Mazar.

Filmography

Film

Year	Title	Role	Notes
1941	Fancy Answers	Girl at Recital	Short film uncredited
1941	Strange Testament	Waitress	Short film uncredited
1941	Shadow of the Thin Man	Passerby	uncredited
1941	H.M. Pulham, Esq.	Young Socialite	uncredited
1941	Babes on Broadway	Audience member	uncredited
1942	Joe Smith, American	Miss Maynard, Secretary	uncredited
1942	This Time for Keeps	Girl in car lighting cigarette	uncredited
1942	We Do It Because	Lucretia Borgia	Short film uncredited

1942   Kid Glove Killer Car Hopuncredited

1942   Sunday Punch   Ringsider   uncredited

1942   Calling Dr. Gillespie   Student at finishing school
        uncredited

1942   Mighty Lak a Goat   Girl at the Bijou box office
        Short film   uncredited

1942   Reunion in France   Marie, a salesgirl
        uncredited

1943   Du Barry Was a Lady   Perfume Girluncredited

1943   Hitler's Madman   Franciska Pritric, a Student
uncredited

1943   Ghosts on the Loose   Betty

1943   Young Ideas   Co-ed   uncredited

1943   Swing Fever   Receptionist uncredited

1943   Lost Angel   Hat Check Girl   uncredited

1944   Two Girls and a Sailor   Dream Girl   uncredited

1944   Three Men in White   Jean Brown

1944   Maisie Goes to Reno   Gloria Fullerton

1944   Blonde Fever   Bit Role   uncredited

1945   She Went to the Races   Hilda Spotts

1946   Whistle Stop   Mary

1946   The Killers   Kitty Collins

1947   The Hucksters   Jean Ogilvie

1947   Singapore   Linda Grahame / Ann Van Leyden

1948   One Touch of Venus   Venus

1949   The Bribe   Elizabeth Hintten

1949   The Great Sinner   Pauline Ostrovsky

1949   East Side, West Side   Isabel Lorrison

1951   Pandora and the Flying Dutchman   Pandora Reynolds

1951   My Forbidden Past   Barbara Beaurevel

1951   Show Boat   Julie LaVerne

1952   Lone Star   Martha Ronda

1952   The Snows of Kilimanjaro   Cynthia Green

1953   The Band Wagon   herself   uncredited

1953   Ride, Vaquero!   Cordelia Cameron

1953   Mogambo   Honey Bear Kelly   nominated – Academy Award for Best Actress

1953   Knights of the Round Table   Guinevere

1954   The Barefoot Contessa   Maria Vargas

1956   Bhowani Junction   Victoria Jones   nominated – BAFTA for Best Foreign Actress

1957   The Little Hut   Lady   Susan Ashlow

1957   The Sun Also Rises   Lady Brett Ashley

1958   The Naked Maja   Maria Cayetana, Duchess of Alba

1959   On the Beach   Moira Davidson   nominated – BAFTA for Best Foreign Actress

1960   The Angel Wore Red   Soledad

1963   55 Days at Peking   Baroness Natalie Ivanoff

1964   Seven Days in May   Eleanor Holbrook

1964   The Night of the Iguana Maxine Faulk   nominated – BAFTA for Best Foreign Actress   nominated – Golden Globe for Best Motion Picture Actress – Drama

1966   The Bible: In the Beginning...   Sarah

1968   Mayerling   Empress Elizabeth

1970   Tam-LinMichaela Cazaret

1972   The Life and Times of Judge Roy Bean   Lily Langtry

1974   Earthquake   Remy Royce-Graff

1975   Permission to Kill   Katina Petersen

1976   The Blue Bird   Luxury

1976   The Cassandra Crossing Nicole Dressler

1977   The Sentinel   Miss Logan

1979	City on Fire	Maggie Grayson
1980	The Kidnapping of the President	Beth Richards
1981	Priest of Love	Mabel Dodge Luhan
1982	Regina Roma	Mama

TV

Year	Title	Role	Notes
1985	A.D.	Agrippina	Miniseries
1985	Knots Landing	Ruth Galveston	7 episodes
1985	The Long Hot Summer	Minnie Littlejohn	TV movie
1986	Harem	Kadin	TV movie
1986	Maggie	Diane Webb	TV movie, (final film role)

Further reading

Cannon, Doris Rollins. Grabtown Girl: Ava Gardner's North Carolina Childhood and Her Enduring Ties to Home. Down Home Press, 2001; ISBN 1-878086-89-8

Fowler, Karin. Ava Gardner: A Bio-Bibliography. Greenwood Press, 1990; ISBN 0-313-26776-6

Gardner, Ava. Ava: My Story. Bantam, 1990; ISBN 0-553-07134-3

Gigliotti, Gilbert, editor. Ava Gardner: Touches of Venus. Entasis Press, 2010; ISBN 978-0-9800999-5-9

Grobel, Lawrence. "Conversations with Ava Gardner", CreateSpace; August 31, 2014.

Rivers, Alton. Love, Ava: A Novel. St. Martin's Press, 2007; ISBN 0-312-36279-X

Server, Lee. Ava Gardner: Love is Nothing. St. Martin's Press, 2006; ISBN 0-312-31209-1

Mims, Bryan. "Our Ava", Our State Magazine, 2014

Wayne, Jane Ellen. Ava's Men: The Private Life of Ava Gardner. Robson Books, 2004; ISBN 1-86105-785-7

If an essay were to be written on the disadvantages of physical superiority, Ava Gardner would've made a perfect test case. Her beauty distracted others, having been an invitation, a property that never seemed her own possession, which might've been lost through an accident. It made men act crazily but made people forgive her. It was something that age would take and that she could ruin, with all those late nights, with all that drink. Above all else, it made her lonely. Gardner wasn't so much herself, as the sum total of other people's reactions to her. She was reduced to being an object, a thing of pure physicality.

Al Altman, who carried out her screen-test, had seen enough starlets to know that a really beautiful woman was rare indeed, being a "freak" of nature. The actor Howard Duff described her as the "most beautiful thing he'd ever seen". To others, she was "an extraordinary creature", "the Taj Mahal of beauty". Or she "was like an animal, Ava. The sex thing."

When Howard Hughes suggested that following her 3 previous marriages, it really ought to have been his turn, Gardner replied: "You make it sound like I'm a pony ride at the county fair." The posters for The Barefoot Contessa (1954) advertised her as "The World's Most Beautiful Animal", while in the movie Marius Goring declared: "You are not a woman . . . I only see that you have the body of an animal. A dead animal."

Ava was the most beautiful girl at Rock Ridge High, it having been her looks that took her to Hollywood. She was famous as a beauty before she was famous as an actress. Her best films both celebrated her appearance and responded to it as a problem, almost a fate. They were always making icons of her: all those publicity stills and bathing-beauty snaps, a portrait by Man Ray for Pandora (1951), the ridiculously overblown statue for the graveside scene in The Barefoot Contessa, which ended up in Frank Sinatra's garden until one of his later wives made him throw it out.

Although her appetites were decidedly her own, having been happy to exploit the effect of her fame and glamour, Gardner wasn't able to rise above Hollywood's objectification of her. Even in Lee Server's sympathetic book, her body wasn't quite her own but something between an exhibit in a freak show and a commodity of pure desire.

He listed Ava's measurements (thighs: 19 inches; calves: 13); he described the problems which arose on set due to her erect nipples, while relating the story of a Mexican playboy trying to find a place on her body that had never been kissed: 'I got to the soles of her feet and I said: "I found it!"'. More unusually, Server shared Mickey Rooney's expressive admiration for Ava's 'c*nt', which apparently had the strength and mobility of a mouth but Gardner's inner life receded, leaving anecdotes and mere physical description.

He applied the same treatment to some of the male protagonists, stating that when naked, Frank Sinatra resembled a tuning fork, a metaphor which left one none the wiser until things were more graphically spelled out. A reporter once asked Ava what she saw in Sinatra, a '119 lbs has-been', she blandly replied: 'Well, I'll tell you – 19lbs is cock!'

Broadly speaking, Gardner's life was that of a small-town girl who became a Hollywood star, followed by a hard-drinking rabble-rouser, then finally a grand but rather sad old lady, with a corgi and a maid, living in one of those sadly grand houses in Knightsbridge. In between, she made some pictures. Ava was never very effective: her career happened in the lulls between drinking bouts or marital fights, or simply when she needed to escape from wherever she happened to be living.

Her habits were all bad ones – getting drunk, smashing crockery, picking up handsome but ultimately unappealing men. In Hollywood, Gardner transformed herself into a sassy, worldly-wise 'broad', someone who'd inquire of an English actor asking for a date: 'Do you eat pussy?' Around the same time she said to the Brazilian lyricist Vinicius de Moraes: 'Yes I'm very beautiful, but morally, I stink.'

Ava was being too hard on herself. She pursued her pleasures, broke a few hearts, but most of the men she had sex with were still boasting about it half a century later. Sexually, there seemed to have been little that she didn't try. Gardner travelled, she drank; she hung out in brothels, danced with gypsies, took part in bull-fights, skinny-dipped, and got herself barred from most of the best hotels in Europe. She had lots of fun.

Ava came from North Carolina, the last of 7 children in a poor farming family. Discovered when her photograph was spotted in a New York photo-store window, she was screen-tested then taken to Hollywood, where she spent a few years contracted to MGM, waiting for a break as a leading lady. Gardner filled in the time by getting married, having wed 3 husbands in rapid succession, two of them before she'd starred in a movie, all of them famous.

First was Mickey Rooney, the star of the Andy Hardy pictures, who was effervescently manic, the kind of man who would try to bring the house down during a quiet lunch. As their marriage disintegrated, Howard Hughes appeared on the scene, who saw Ava for what she was about to become: the commodifiable woman, his statement of his intention to marry her – 'I can do no better' – sounding like a strap-line for a car ad. However, Gardner was resistant to the charms of money, refusing to be sold at market.

Ava's 2nd husband was Artie Shaw, the band-leader. While Rooney had looked up to her then Hughes stalked her, Artie tried to educate her. Shaw was an intellectual who oppressed her with psychoanalysis and Buddenbrooks, having made her pack a copy of The Origin of Species to take on honeymoon. As this marriage soon faded out, Gardner made her first significant film, The Killers (1946).

Following Artie came a period of pick-ups and cocktails before Ava fell for Frank Sinatra, who was about to fall to his career low point. In his way, Sinatra was worse than Shaw or Hughes, faking suicide to get back at her, punching photographers, hanging out with the Mafia. Their arguments were the stuff of legend, at first their lovers tiffs being stormy prologues to an equally passionate making-up. However, soon the fights were only fights, it not being long before they couldn't live together at all.

Gardner never remarried after the split with Frank but there were countless lovers, from the guy who did the props to maybe Fidel Castro. Although she had some let downs with sex, in the main her erotic life was a dizzying round of pleasure, Ava spending 20 years doing the female equivalent of 'womanising'. Her serial seductions were sometimes due to sexual desire but at others because of her fear of sleeping alone, some men being invited back to her place just to keep her company. Gardner's longest Hollywood affair post-Sinatra was with George C. Scott, the worst of all her lovers.

Ava had little private life, her failed marriage to Frank having inspired 'In the Wee Small Hours of the Morning', one of the great heartbreak records. Nelson Riddle said that Sinatra's voice during this period was 'like a cello . . . Ava taught him the hard way.' Frank transformed his 'private life' and, more importantly, the publicity about it, back into public art, Gardner doing the same, the process being the key to her career.

Her affair with Sinatra, who was married when they met, briefly turned Ava into a public hate figure, before she changed perceptions, following her performance as a sad, deserted woman in Show Boat (1951). Both beautiful and tortured, Gardner became someone the audience could love, the scripts of her films began to refer to a back catalogue of affairs and to her increasing notoriety as a drunk.

At first, Hollywood hadn't known what to do with her, so she waited for something to happen. Ava was groomed, she was photographed, but avoided being coerced onto the casting couch, so she was put in many low-budget quickies, including Ghosts on the Loose, a forerunner of Scooby Doo, but without the wit and sophistication.

Then came The Killers, a dreary and portentous movie, a pseudo-tough version of Citizen Kane, Gardner not being at her best as a femme fatale. Barbara Stanwyck could play the chilling tramp, and Veronica Lake was a charming blank, but Ava just looked like a nice kid from North Carolina who'd got herself into trouble. Although she may in later life have become scary and fiery company, she was essentially just too nice, which The Killers couldn't avoid revealing.

Gardner's strength emerged as just being herself on screen, her repeated insistence that she wasn't an actress not having been false modesty. When she came to play Pandora she read the description of her character – 'Complex, moody, restless with the discontent of a romantic soul which hasn't yet found the true object of her desires' then said: 'It's almost me.'

When she read the script of The Barefoot Contessa, she told Joseph Mankiewicz: 'I'm not an actress, but I think I understand this girl. She's a lot like me.' Ava's increasing identification with her screen performances wasn't a surprise, it was how the star factory worked. They called Gardner the 'Hollywood Cinderella', but nearly every '50s female Hollywood star was that, the medium itself providing the transformation that turned a Norma-Jean into a Marilyn. The pictures would be not only about her, but about her transformation by film.

Audrey Hepburn's gamine looks were supposed to have made her invisible, it having been for Hollywood to uncover her unusual beauty, hence the revelations of Sabrina or Funny Face. With Ava, it wasn't her extraordinary good looks that were being revealed – her attractiveness being obvious to everyone – but a spirit in her, something hidden behind the beauty, something natural that it'd require a lot of artifice to bring out. The studio set out to remake Gardner, as they set out to remake everyone in those days. Her voice was changed, she was told how to move, all in an attempt to capture a 'quality' that they saw she had anyway. Film would draw out a hidden essence, rendering it as surface: the shiny, beautiful, glow of Technicolor.

In the move from Grabtown, North Carolina to Hollywood, Ava was driven to become something new, a modern creature, freed from the limits that life might've otherwise held for her. She had to play many roles to get by, including the child of nature constrained by the brutality of civilisation, while coming to exemplify a kind of American modernity: the Hemingwayesque life of fast cars, fast planes, bourbon, bull fights and expatriation, rooted in an antique American image – a new direction for old frontier stock. Gardner even played 3 Hemingway heroines, including the love interest in the dire Snows of Kilimanjaro.

Some of the best directors she worked with – Albert Lewin, George Cukor, John Huston – tried to find what they felt was the private, natural quality in her, trying to catch it on film but

Ava, who'd been clearly shy when she was young, was still secretly shy when older, even oddly shy before the camera, so although she always looked pretty, at first she was a wooden performer.

Gardner became an actress when she found a way of presenting herself on screen, that self being in two senses a Hollywood creation: both the kind of person the milieu allowed, and the package sold to the world through her relationship with the press. The quality those directors discovered wasn't the natural woman from Grabtown, but a product of the industry.

Ava conformed with this process, even as she seemed to rebel against it, her rebellions being enacted on screen: the bad behaviour, the drinking, the player's refusal to play. The Cinderella myth had to do with the transformation of ordinariness, what was special about Hollywood stars being that they could be perfectly ordinary and untouchable princesses at the same time.

For the public, the women in those '50s movies existed in a discrepancy between two models of knowledge and intimacy, both manufactured. There was the intimacy of film itself, the close scrutiny and imaginative identification with the star then there was the knowledge provided by the press, the gossip magazines, the newspaper photographs.

Gardner was the model for Anita Ekberg's character in La Dolce Vita, which explained who she'd become in the eyes of the public and the paparazzi. Many of the fake elements that made up Ava's public persona were there: Ekberg's enactment of a wild child given over to pleasure, adored by men, but unattainable by them, strongly sexual, frustratingly innocent, pursued by cameras, while always behaving as though one were

23

there watching her. Only Gardner's saving qualities, her capacity for affection and her genuine warmth, were lacking.

The Barefoot Contessa brilliantly portrayed the process of Ava's immersion in Hollywood, exposing one essential part of the Gardner myth, present with almost every movie star but uniquely strong in her case. The film payed tribute to the impressively egalitarian nature of Ava's sexual desire. Its male stars couldn't have sex with her, being father figures like Bogart, weird like Warren Stevens, or impotent like Rossano Brazzi.

On the other hand, Gardner's character was free to have sex with many anonymous and unseen ordinary men, gypsies, servants, men glimpsed infrequently or kept off screen altogether but she paid for this freedom with her life. The picture responded to the audience's basic desire that the star could still be someone whom any one of them might possess but she also fell victim to the movie's and the viewer's envious moralism, murdered by her stupidly jealous husband. Ava's character was constrained between desire and judgment, precisely the ground she occupied in her media life.

In retrospect her career wasn't a poor one, having outlasted some other promising femmes fatales, including Rita Hayworth or Jane Greer, whose film work was effectively over by the early '50s, her staying power having been her strength. When nearly everyone else of her generation was either dead, retired or in TV, Gardner produced what may've been her best ever performance, in John Huston's adaptation of Tennessee Williams's The Night of the Iguana (1964).

A couple of years later, she wanted to play Mrs Robinson in The Graduate, a perfect piece of casting, sabotaged by Ava's self-doubt and reluctance to strip. She was in many bad or dull movies, though she also made some good ones, including Pandora, Mogambo (1953), The Barefoot Contessa, Bhowani Junction (1956) and The Night of the Iguana. However, Gardner was never in a truly great picture, her performances somehow failing to add up to an oeuvre.

Ava Gardner had been dead for 20 years, remembered as a film star of flawless beauty and a love goddess of infinite scandal. Once described as 'the most irresistible woman in Hollywood', she epitomised its golden years. Although she'd seldom been accused of great acting, she'd seduced, been seduced by, married and divorced, lived with and walked out on, some of the most famous names of the 20th century, having had toyboys before Cher had toys.

'My vices and scandals are more interesting than anything anyone can make up,' Ava said in 1988, when starting work on her autobiography. She was essentially a private person, so it was a book she never really wanted to write: 'I'm broke, honey,' Gardner said when asked why she was finally prepared to tell her story. 'I either write the book or sell the jewels, and I'm kinda sentimental about the jewels.' However, the book never saw the light of day.

Ava was 66 years old, living in her apartment in Knightsbridge, London, wearing nothing but an angry scowl and a bath towel, partly because she wanted to see how one would react to her state of dishabille, never to her dying day having lost her pride in her sexuality. 'I loathe it when people spread bedtime stories about me. I was just in the tub when a friend called from LA.

She said that Marlon Brando told her he'd once slept with me. That's a god damn lie!'

Gardner went on to say that she'd called Marlon about it straightaway. If he'd really believed they'd ever been lovers, she'd told him angrily, his brain had gone soft. Brando had apologised, saying that his brain wasn't the only part of his anatomy that had gone soft lately. 'Isn't that punishment enough, Ava?' he'd lisped. Disarmed, and amused, by his frankness, she'd largely forgiven him.

'I don't know about Jimmy Dean, Ingrid Bergman, Larry Olivier, Jackie Onassis, and the rest of the names Marlon's supposed to have carved on his bedpost, but my name's definitely not one of them, honey. I know that a lot of men fantasise about me, but that's how Hollywood gossip becomes Hollywood history. Someday someone's going to say, "All the lies ever told about Ava Gardner are true," then the truth about me, just like the truth about poor, maligned Marilyn Monroe, will disappear like names on old tombstones.

I know I'm not exactly defending a spotless reputation. Hell, it's way too late for that. Scratching one name off my dance-card won't mean a row of beans in the final tally. It's just that I like to keep the books straight while I'm still around and sufficiently sober and compos mentis to do it,' Gardner said.

Although her fine cheekbones still gave her face a sculptural force, two years earlier she'd had a stroke, which had partially paralysed her left side, freezing half her face in a rictus of sadness. It would've been a hard blow to bear for any woman, but for an actress who'd been hailed as 'the world's most beautiful animal', it was a tragedy.

26

'As if getting old wasn't tough enough, but life doesn't stop because you're no longer beautiful. You just have to make adjustments. Although I'd be lying to you if I told you that losing my looks is no big deal. It hurts, god damn it, it hurts like a son-of-a-bitch. The thing is, I survived, and I have to be grateful for that. You're just reminded of your mortality. You go on living, knowing that from now on death is always close at hand. It's been an interesting life; I've had a wonderful time, in parts. Certainly I'd be crazy to start squawking now.'

I got my great skin and energy from Mama, and my shyness, my sense of privacy and green eyes from Daddy. He always called me Daughter, never Ava. He worked hard all his life, but you knew he was never going to be a rich man. He was a gentle man, a bit of a dreamer. Like me, he sometimes drank too much, and smoked too much. He died of bronchitis when I was 13. I missed him more than I ever thought it was possible to miss anyone.'

Ava was 18, heading for a career as a shorthand-typist, when her sister Beatrice, nicknamed Bappie, invited her to New York for the Thanksgiving holiday. By this time, she'd grown into a striking, natural beauty, Bappie's husband, Larry Tarr, a professional photographer, being stunned by her looks, telling her prophetically, 'You oughta be in pictures'.

Larry displayed one of his portraits of her in the window of his Fifth Avenue photographic shop, which was noticed by an office boy from Loew's Inc, a subsidiary of Metro-Goldwyn-Mayer, named Barney Duhan. Hoping to finagle a date with the shop-window beauty, Duhan called the store, posing as an MGM talent scout, to ask for Gardner's telephone number. The manager refused to give it to him but passed on his query to

Tarr, who believing it to be a serious inquiry, sent Ava's pictures to MGM's New York office.

Her pictures landed on the desk of a genuine executive, who sent for Ava, being impressed by her looks but unable to understand 'more than a couple of words of what I said: my accent was pure Tobacco Road South, honey', shrewdly ordering a silent screen test to send to Hollywood. 'I had less than no experience, I didn't know anything about anything, but part of me always knew that one day I'd be a movie queen. Anyway, I certainly didn't have a hell of a lot to lose. What was the alternative - a secretary's job in Sleepy Hollow? When they told me that MGM was where Clark Gable worked, my mind was made up,' Gardner reflected.

Chaperoned by her big sister, Ava caught the train to Hollywood to 'put myself in play'. A sound test detected no star potential, with her almost incomprehensible Southern drawl having seemed to condemn her to a bleak future in Hollywood. Fortunately for her, all the studios kept pools of talentless pretty girls under contract, for decorating studio functions, entertaining visiting VIPs, and for walk-on parts. In the summer of 1941, aged 18, Gardner was signed to a 7-year contract starting at $50 / week.

'I spent most of my time in what they called Leg Art Alley, where photographers did nothing but take publicity stills for newspapers and magazines. It was part of the regular grooming programme and I didn't like it one bit, but it kept me looking busy, so they didn't drop my option.' Determined to lose her Southern drawl - 'I didn't know I had an accent until I got to

Hollywood and people laughed at the way I spoke' - Ava took all the voice lessons she could get.

It was the beginning of what she called 'the long epiphany of the rest of my life' - the transformation of the shy Southern hillbilly into one of the most notorious and glamorous movie sirens in Hollywood. The first star Gardner met at MGM was Mickey Rooney, who was in character for a movie, dressed in a Brazilian drag costume, his mouth smeared with lipstick, looking ludicrous, but it didn't stop him from asking Ava for a date.

Rooney was the biggest star on the MGM lot - more famous than Spencer Tracy, bigger than Clark Gable, but 6 inches shorter than Ava, who was impressed, but smart enough to turn him down. She called it Rule Number One of the Southern Lady Conventions: a lady must be courted - and a gentleman must be patient.

Mickey was persistent, being smitten, having begun proposing to her on a regular basis until Gardner gave in - with one proviso: 'Not until I'm 19, honey!' Rooney settled for that. 'Well, I guess he ain't been able to get into your pants yet,' his mother told Ava when they first broke the news to her. Ma Rooney knew her son well; Gardner was still a virgin when they married on January 10th, 1942. A year and 5 days later, following public brawls and rumours of Ava's intemperate conjugal demands they were divorced: 'I owe Mickey something: through him I discovered that I enjoyed sex,' Gardner said later.

Although Ava's looks made her a byword for Hollywood glamour, her career was still going nowhere, before she married the virtuoso clarinettist and male chauvinist Artie Shaw during 1945. 'Artie was an intellectual, I was smart but I had no education at all - we were made for each other,' she said later.

Determined to educate Gardner, Shaw told her to read more books - 'you can't listen to Frank Sinatra records all the time,' he told her; having hated Sinatra's voice.

She bought the bestseller of the day, but when he found her reading Forever Amber, Artie was furious, declaring 'I won't have a wife of mine reading that rubbish,' hurling the bodice-ripping novel right across the room. A year after they wed, Ava and Shaw were divorced. Ironically, Artie's next wife was Kathleen Winsor, who'd written Forever Amber. Gardner went on to marry her third and last husband, Frank Sinatra.

Hollywood's top boss, Louis B. Mayer, hushed up scandals including the night Howard Hughes dislocated her jaw and she felled him with a marble ashtray. Ava thought she'd killed him, saying 'There was blood on the walls, on the furniture, real blood in the Bloody Marys. Mr Mayer sent in his henchmen to clean up the place and get me out of there fast. He feared it might become a murder scene. I don't think he cared too much about me, but he didn't want any scandal attached to his studio.'

Hughes recovered, having asked Gardner to marry him but the mix was too volatile, having said: 'Our chemistry was the stuff that causes hydrogen bombs to explode. Til death do us part would've been a whole lot sooner than later if we'd tied the knot. Howard was a control freak, and I was too independent to take his crap. He was out of his mind most of the time, even then, and he got crazier through the years.'

Although she made no impact in any of the dozen b-movies she made at MGM, an outside studio borrowed her to play George Raft's sultry squeeze in a minor noir thriller, Whistle Stop: 'That was my first leading role. George Raft was old enough to be my father [aged 43]. He took some handling, but I adored him.' Her performance led to her being cast in the role of Burt Lancaster's double-crossing girlfriend in The Killers.

'Whatever it is, whether you're born with it, or catch it from a public drinking cup, she's got it,' Humphrey Bogart said when he saw the performance, recognising the quality that makes a star. Director Joseph Mankiewicz lifted the line straight from Bogart to describe Ava in The Barefoot Contessa, the story of a gypsy dancer discovered by a film director, played by Bogart, being turned into a Hollywood legend.

Gardner's marriage to Frank Sinatra lasted under 6 years but, in a sadomasochistic way, their romance never ended. Outspoken, caustic and often wickedly funny, Ava relished talking about the past, her highs and lows, her indiscretions, her mistakes. Nothing was spared - until she saw it on the page: 'Jesus Christ, we can't publish this!' Ava, it's your life. 'Exactly, honey!'.

'My body's failing every which way,' she said later after stumbling in her apartment. She walked with a cane; once a heavy smoker, she had pulmonary emphysema, the lung disease that had recently killed her one-time lover, the director John Huston. Gardner didn't see many people, but hated being called a recluse: 'I'm just winding down, honey. It's been a long haul from Grabtown. I'm just taking a little time out. I'm entitled to that,' she said shortly before she died during January, 1990.

"I thought I was making $50 a week [at MGM], but it turned out to be $35, because 12 weeks of the year you were on layoff. It was white slavery, and it lasted for 17 years."

31

"We hadn't been married 5 minutes when he decided I should go to an analyst. Artie was a pseudo-intellectual. He had a great oral diarrhea. I was constantly being put down. I was madly in love with him, but I wasn't treated as an equal, as a wife; I was treated as sort of his little pet."

"I dealt with men who had tempers, and who could get violent—Lord knows how I had to defend myself against Howard Hughes and Frank Sinatra, and from Artie Shaw's verbal abuse, but George [C. Scott] was a different category of animal when he got drunk. He'd break into my hotel room, which he did in Italy, London and at the Beverly Hills Hotel, attack me to where I was frightened for my life, and scream, 'Why won't you marry me?' Well, I would never marry a man who couldn't control his liquor. Me, I'm a happy drunk. I laugh, I dance. I certainly don't break bottles and threaten to kill."

On Sinatra: "The poor guy was literally without a job. He said all he could do was play saloons and crappy night clubs. His ego and self-esteem was at its lowest ever but mine was practically at its peak. So it was hell for him. He was such a proud man -- to have a woman pay all his bills was a bitch."

"I was lazy. I would've been a hell of a lot better actress had I taken it more seriously. I never had the proper respect for acting. Quite often, I learned my lines on the way to the studio."

"I didn't know anything about him. I didn't know about his reputation or his great wealth or his thing about airplanes and jetting around the world. I just knew that as soon as I got divorced from Mickey, Howard entered my life and I couldn't get rid of him for the next 15 years, no matter who I was with or who I married."

On 'The Killers': "Oh, what the hell did I know? I went to the set the first day in full makeup and the director told me to take it off. So I did the film without makeup. I had nothing to do with anything I did. I never understood why I was so famous."

On Marlon Brando: "We went back to his hotel and had some drinks. I wasn't wearing a bra and he reached over and grabbed my breasts and said, 'Are those real?' I said, 'I believe they are.'"

On Mickey Rooney: "He came to visit me at the hospital and I heard the Jesus Christ routine. He's a reborn Christian. He kept on about being made in the image of God. What a load of crap!"

"Some of the things that I regret most in my life happened when I was drinking. I'm just not good with alcohol and I don't give a damn what time of the day it is, I just drink too much."

91